Jefferson
Davis
Gets His
Citizenship
Back

Jefferson Davis Gets His Citizenship Back

ROBERT PENN WARREN

THE UNIVERSITY PRESS OF KENTUCKY

The University Press of Kentucky is the
scholarly publisher for the Commonwealth,
serving Berea College, Centre College of Kentucky,
Eastern Kentucky University, The Filson Club,
Georgetown College, Kentucky Historical Society,
Kentucky State University, Morehead State University,
Murray State University, Northern Kentucky University,
Transylvania University, University of Kentucky,
University of Louisville, and Western Kentucky University.

Editorial and Sales Offices: Lexington, Kentucky 40506

ISBN: 0-8131-1445-4
Library of Congress Catalog Card Number: 80-51023

Jefferson
Davis
Gets His
Citizenship
Back

THERE are two kinds of memory. One is narrative, the unspooling in the head of what has happened, like a movie film with no voices. The other is symbolic—the image, say, of a dead friend of long ago, with a characteristic expression of face, which may be called up by a name. When I think of my maternal grandfather, I see an old man with white hair and a rather pointed beard, wearing bluejean pants, with a black tie hanging loose from a collar open at the throat—for in that memory it is an unchanging summer. He is sitting in a sturdy split-bottom chair, with its arms broadening to wide, rounded ends—the kind of chair that in the old days appeared here and there among rockers of similar design on the verandas of summer hotels in the South, called springs, where people went to avoid malaria. But my grandfather's chair is under a cedar tree, propped back against the trunk, and blue smoke from his cob pipe threads thinly upward into the darkness of the cedar.

I am a small boy sitting tailor-fashion on the unkempt lawn, looking up at the old man, and then, beyond him, at the whitewashed board fence, and then at the woods coming down almost to the fence. If it was getting toward sunset, the uncountable guinea fowl would be coming in from foraging to roost near the house, making a metallic and disgruntled but halfhearted clatter, not the full, outraged racket of morning. I would be waiting for the old man to talk. Or even to sing, in his old, cracked voice, one of the few songs that might rise from his silence, sung only for himself. "We'll Gather in the Canebrake and Hunt the Buffalo"—but even then I knew that long before his father's time the buffalo had found their classic habitat on the Great Plains out West. Or a sad song about "Hallie in the Valley," which I later learned was the song the Confederate troops had sung down the streets of New Orleans to wind up at Shiloh. And there was the song that began, "I wandered today to the hill, Maggie," which, like the others, seemed to be backward-looking. For, in spite of the obvious knowledge that I would grow up, I had the sweet-sad feeling that the world had already happened, that history had come to an end—though life did go on, and people lived, died, went broke.

Certainly that sense of changelessness hung over the run-down farm and farmhouse and under the cedar tree. My grandfather had lost his wife, Mary, years back. His only son lived far off in Atlanta. His daughters were all married and gone far away—except the "beauty," that is, who was now an old maid, and the youngest one, who remained there on the farm to keep house for the old man. She was a small, charming woman, full of gaiety, vigorous and competent. She could pick up a twelve-gauge by the kitchen door, step out on the back porch, and knock a chicken hawk out of the sky—all in one motion, it seemed—and step back in and resume whatever song she had been singing. And she had the spunk to stand up to her father's awe-inspiring opposition to the man of her choice and run away and marry anyway—at the house of my parents, in the small town of Guthrie, Kentucky.

Then the old man let the new husband take over the running of the farm, and sought refuge in his books as long as his eyes held out. In the summer, when the married daughters came for a visit under his roof, and I came, too, I might hear them now and then remark, "Papa is an inveterate reader"—which I understood as "Confederate reader," wondering all the while what a Confederate reader might be. The daughters might say, too, "Papa is not practical, he is visionary." And this, I gradually learned, referred to his one venture as a businessman, years back, when he had apparently been fairly successful as a tobacco buyer but, if I have the family talk right, had forgotten to pay an insurance premium on a warehouse of tobacco consigned to him, and the warehouse, such was his luck, burned. I remember hearing my young aunt and her husband singing together night after night, out in a swing on the lawn, in darkness or by moonlight, and seeing the streak of lamplight under my grandfather's door. He would be reading. All this long after I was supposed to be asleep.

Nobody ever came to the farm—through "the big gate," a mile off on the pike—except kin and a family named Rawls: a widow with two daughters and a son, my only playmate. The Rawlses would come twice a summer, for late Sunday dinner, and always after dinner the older daughter (who studied "elocution" and later became a college professor) would give a "recital," with gestures and stances, of poems my grandfather liked. His own head was, in fact, full of poems, and under the cedar he would sometimes begin reciting to me. There might be the stirring lines of Fitz-Greene Halleck's "Marco Bozzaris":

At midnight, in his guarded tent,
    The Turk was dreaming of the hour
When Greece, her knee in suppliance
        bent,
    Should tremble at his power.

On to the surprise attack by Bozzaris and his exhortation:

Strike—for the green graves of your
        sires;
    God—and your native land!

Byron usually followed: "So, We'll Go No More a-Roving" and bits of "Childe Harold." And always Burns, in the old man's version of the Scots tongue. But I remember, too, the expression of pitiful outrage when memory would leave him stranded with some eloquence already on his lips.

5

What I liked even better than the poetry, however, was the random tale of a war he himself had fought for four years. He had volunteered as a private but by Shiloh was a captain of cavalry, and in that rank remained. He was—for a time, at least—under the immediate command of General James Ronald Chalmers; Chalmers was later attached to General Nathan B. Forrest, the old man's hero. His account of the war came in bits and pieces, sometimes bloody, sometimes funny. My grandfather was not a witty man, but he could boast of one retort that, after all the years, still pleased his vanity. In northern Mississippi, a patrol from his company surprised a Yankee patrol and brought in, among the survivors, a lieutenant who was rather swarthy but not Negroid. He spoke a very correct English, but with a strange accent. My grandfather asked what he was. He was a Turk, he replied, and my grandfather demanded what, in God's name, he was doing in Mississippi. "I am here to learn the art of war," the Turk replied proudly. My grandfather remarked that he had come to the right place.

By no means all tales were comic. He had been outside Fort Pillow, on the Mississippi River north of Memphis, when Forrest sent in a demand for surrender, ending with the statement that without surrender "I cannot be responsible for the fate of your command." But the men of the Union garrison felt snug in there, the old man said, and they had a gunboat, too. (It also turned out, apparently, that the fort's liquor supply was to become available.) The ramparts were built too wide for the defending artillery on top to lower muzzles to guard the fort's moat, however; a solid curtain of hot lead from the rifles of sharpshooters stationed in convenient woods swept it clean of gunners while the attackers scaled the wall over a bridge of human backs in the moat and poured in; the garrison panicked, and the blue command went into such a funk that formal surrender was impossible. A great many men of the garrison, fleeing down the bluff to the protection of the gunboat—protection that was not forthcoming, since the men inside were afraid of opening the gunports—were cut down by rifle fire. Some of the men tried to surrender individually— often with little success, especially if they were black.

The river ran red, the old man told me, but he didn't say that the battle was termed a massacre in the Northern press and in Congress, and that Lincoln ordered an investigation, so that retaliation could be made. General William T. Sherman was put in charge of the investigation, but eventually came to the conclusion that there was no ground for retaliation, even though the ratio of black troops killed among the defenders was definitely higher than that of white. Forrest had made every personal effort to stop the slaughterous disorder.

Generally, however, my grandfather's accounts were more abstract, and concerned tactics and strategy, with now and then a battle plan scratched on the ground with the point of his stick, and orders for me to move empty rifle shells to demonstrate an action for his explanation. Not always were these battles of the Civil War, for a book that he read over and over was "Napoleon and His Marshals" (by J. T. Headley, published in 1846), and the battle plan on the ground might be that of Austerlitz or Lodi.

Time seemed frozen, because nothing seemed to be happening there on

8

that remote farm except the same things again and again: there where nobody came, and newspapers meant nothing to me—not even the one my grandfather held in his hand while he read the headlines about the beginning of the First World War, before he crumpled it, and said, "The sons of bitches are at it again."

In the ever-present history there was, however, a kind of puzzlement. I had picked up a vaguely soaked-in popular notion of the Civil War, the wickedness of Yankees, the justice of the Southern cause (whatever it was; I didn't know), the slave question, with Lincoln somehow a great man but misguided. The impression of the Civil War certainly did not come from my own household, where the war was rarely mentioned, and where, aside from poetry, what my father read to the children was history—a "Child's History of Greece" or a "Child's History of Rome," and, later, a history of France (with a red cover). No, I didn't get my impression of the Civil War from home. I got it from the air around me (with the ambiguous Lincoln bit probably from a schoolroom). But my old grandfather, who *was* history, was often a shock to my fuddled preoccupations.

One afternoon, I almost jumped out of my skin when he musingly remarked that he had been a Union man. That is, he went on, he had been against secession—hadn't wanted to see the country his folks had had a good hand in making (his folks, it later developed, had been Virginians) split up and get "Balkanized." I didn't know what the word meant, but he explained. Then he told me that his Great-Grandfather Abram had been a colonel in the Revolution, and an uncle (or was it a cousin of the same generation?) had signed the Declaration. The old man also said he had known that slavery couldn't last—even if I gathered from conversation that there must have been slaves in the family. For instance, I knew Old Aunt Cat, who had been my grandfather's nurse (and was to outlive him about twenty years), and who, I was told, had come with the family when they fled from Tennessee to Kentucky. But he said that when war came "you went with your people." Sometimes, however, in speaking of the war in a different tone, he would call it "a politicians' war." Or say, "It didn't have to be. It was just worked up by fools—Southern fire-eaters and Yankee abolitionists." Perhaps he merely expected history to be rational—that most irrational of expectations.

For a long time, I have wondered how truly his random recollections corresponded to the views that he had held as a young volunteer. He was a loner, a man of great independence of mind, and a man who, though he must have considered himself a failure, maintained a dignity and self-assurance almost amounting to contempt for the way the world wagged or the cards fell. He even deplored segregation, simply because he felt it stupid and restrictive of his own freedom.

There was the question of Jefferson Davis. In my shadowy understanding of history, I assumed that since Jefferson Davis had been President of the Confederacy he was beyond reproach. But not for my grandfather—he could come close to saying right out that Jeff had thrown the war away. My first puzzlement arose, I imagine, from the fact that he called the President merely Jeff. When I was a small boy, there was a walking monument to Jef-

ferson Davis back in my home town—
years before the great monolith that
now looms some miles to the north had
been set up. This man, this walking
monument, may have been named for
the President of the Confederacy, for
he was born in the middle of Reconstruction. He may even have been a
kinsman, though my efforts to find
some connection between him and the
numberless siblings of Jefferson Davis
have come to nothing, and I remember
reading that there were two families
named Davis in the early days of the
county. This walking monument was
always called Old Jeff Davis—the
"Old" being almost part of his name,
not because of years but because he
seemed to have no age. The lowest of
the low, insofar as a white man could
reach that point—a feckless handyman
who owned a rusty hammer and a bent
T-square and no skill whatsoever—he
was stunted, twisted, clad in scarcely
identifiable rags, with an old black felt
hat, greened by age and weather,
usually pulled down to pin in place
large ears; he had no real beard but a
face always unshaven in some scraggly
fashion, cob pipe held uncertainly in

place by stubs of teeth as brown as cured tobacco.

I vaguely remember his shack, improvised from odds and ends, probably—old lard cans beaten out flat, two-by-fours, windows scrounged somewhere, a gutted mattress in the grassless yard, and, no doubt, a broken china chamber pot. The shack faced on the railroad track, out toward the "nigger" graveyard called Vinegar Hill, and on Saturday afternoons years back you'd see Old Jeff Davis plodding down the track, an empty croker sack flagging at his back, to bring home the next week's "traden"—the source of the purchase price of which was anybody's wild guess, and also the price of the rotgut that, I remember, often tempered the aroma of unwashedness in which he moved as in an invisible cloud. Down the track would follow "Mrs. Jeff," squaw-fashion, footing the ties, and then a train of "young'uns," dwindling in size to a struggling toddler. Sometimes Mrs. Jeff celebrated the occasion by tying a pink or red ribbon around the man's straw field hat she always wore. A string of snuff juice trailed out of a corner of her mouth and over her seamed and nearly snuff-colored skin.

In early times when I sat with my grandfather (I was six when I first spent a summer with him), I was puzzled about the relation between the Davis who had lived in a world of great events and my Old Jeff, whose name had entered into the common speech of the region: "as pore as Old Jeff Davis." Could they be the same? The world-shaker dwindled to this? Bit by bit, however, things sorted themselves out, and the deficiencies of the world-shaker began to have some documentation. There was the idiotic favoritism he showed toward certain generals. (They included Braxton Bragg, only a name to me then except for my grandfather's description of him as a "pedantic fool"—with some trouble in explaining the word "pedantic" to me. He had no need, though, to explain the more damning words that before a battle Bragg had "as much fighting heart as a sick pussycat.") I learned, too, that Davis neglected the West and lost Vicksburg; that he failed to recognize, in time to do any good, the genius of General Forrest, the one man who might have handled Sherman. But

I remember, too, my grandfather's saying once or twice that Davis was "a gentleman" and that personally he had had "the courage of a man."

I can't say how my early brand of uninstructed Southernism soaked into me—the kind that got shocked by many things my grandfather said. I can scarcely believe that it came from the atmosphere of the town where I was born—Guthrie—which was, except in geography, anything but an old Southern town. The autochthonous little settlements in the region had been gradually absorbed when a Louisville & Nashville Railroad crossing started a small-scale realtor's dream: ground measured out and the map of a hypothetical town flung down on a pretty countryside of woodlots and woods, streams, ponds, pastures, and fields of corn or tobacco, with old farmsteads, some handsome, some with modest charm, and also—it should be, in candor, noted—a number of tumbledown shacks of tenantry, black and white.

By and large, Guthrie was a railroad town, without a sense of belonging in any particular place or having any particular history. No, it did have one fleeting brush with history. On

September 24, 1904, Felix Grundy Ewing, of Glenraven, Tennessee, called a meeting at the Guthrie fairgrounds and race track to organize the Dark Tobacco Protective Association, later the Planters' Protective Association of Kentucky, Tennessee, and Virginia. Some five to six thousand growers responded, who with kin and onlookers numbered, it was said in my childhood, some twenty-five thousand people. (I have an old photograph of the scene: buggies hub to hub, horsemen so packed together that legs were crushed between mounts—as far as eye, or camera, could see.) The growers were being driven to desperation by a price-fixing conspiracy among the big companies. The association was in the right, but it developed, unofficially, a violent wing, the Night Riders, which, in its most adventurous exploit, in the middle of the night, with military precision, took the neighboring "big" town of Hopkinsville, cut all wires, occupied the railroad-telegraph office and the telephone office, and systematically dynamited all the warehouses of the companies. Before and after this, whippings, barn burnings, and killings were a commonplace, for violence in a "good"

16

cause had led to mere violence. Then came martial law. One of my earliest recollections is of being held up in my father's arms to watch the National Guard set up an encampment in Guthrie, down by the railroad station. Peace was restored. And the courts, after the jog of violence, finally acted to break up the conspiracy to fix prices.

Life settled down into small-town routine, with the major excitement the almost annual fight between a new school principal and the biggest bully among the pupils. I recall that one year a frail-looking new principal dramatically, with what amounted to karate expertise, threw Charlie Parham, who probably had fifty pounds on the assailant, through the glass of a window fifteen feet above ground. Charlie, a good-natured oaf, turned up the next morning smiling, saying, "I thought the son of a bitch was coming right after me, so I hit running and ran all the way to town." A few doting fathers, in similar instances, brought suit against winners, but regularly lost. In an instance before my time, so James Groves (clerk of the Circuit and District Courts and past president of the county historical society) writes me, the

17

locomotive of the little evening train for the seven miles from Elkton to Guthrie, bearing news of the day's legal proceedings and the person of the lately accused pedagogue, burst into wild toots of triumph to celebrate acquittal and law and order. Another year, a boy in the tenth grade (my grade then) flattened a street-carnival hand with a tent peg, was tried for murder, was acquitted on the ground of self-defense, and came back to school to bask in his glory—but this is now memory, for Groves tells me that the records of any such incident, if there ever were any, cannot be found. The days of semi-frontier violence were, however, soon to pass. When the First World War began, male principals were called to the colors, and a stern female professional of middle age and little mercy took over. The germ of primitive chivalry lurking in the breast of local roughs did the rest.

By this time, Guthrie was beginning to doubt its own future, for fewer and fewer trains were stopping, and some even dashed contemptuously through. The automobile was beginning to destroy the "Sat'dy traden" of a market town in favor of trips to larger and more glamorous places, which for the first time were now seeming close. What sense of history had existed in the region was in the old farm families, who had long memories. (One old man—my brother's father-in-law, in fact—used to tell how his father had ridden off wearing the gray, a body servant following on a second horse with a little trunk of fresh clothes and such things on the crupper.) In addition to long memories, a number of the farmers had a strong civic sense, and were sometimes bookish. One whom I knew very well—he was a rarity, I confess—would now and then take a university student who was about to fail Greek and tutor him all summer, just to keep his own hand in, he would say; the "boy" would have four hours of tutorial and four hours of physical labor. In later years, I met one of the boys when he arrived on his pious annual pilgrimage to see the old man who had "made" his life for him—the boy now a sartorially impressive figure and an impressive member of the bar in Chicago.

I remember, in childhood, being taken by my family in a rented surrey to spend a weekend in the house of farm friends, and, when I was older, going out alone for a weekend or so. Perhaps in those days I picked up the Southernism that my grandfather now and then shocked. No reference to Jefferson Davis sticks in my mind from that period, however, and the visits to the farms ceased as the older people died off, leaving my family in a contracting circle.

Toward the time I was ten or eleven, I began to hear the name of Jefferson Davis on the streets. This was scarcely a symptom of Southern chauvinism. There was "news" in the name of Davis now. The news was that, not many miles off, in the settlement of Fairview, a big monument was going to be erected to Jefferson Davis, whoever the hell he was—a monument taller, maybe, than the Washington Monument. A monument meant jobs—even if the First World War, before our entry, was already spurring the American economy. It meant jobs with no questions asked about the color of the uniform your grandfather had worn, or even whether he had been a bushwhacker. In truth, such questions had never been of burning importance in Guthrie, where to a certain number of contemporary citizens the Civil

War seemed to have been fought for the right to lynch without legal interference.

The monument project had been in the air for some time. In 1907, remnants of the Kentucky "Orphan Brigade"—Confederate troops drawn from a state that had not declared for the Confederacy—had organized the Jefferson Davis Memorial Association, which took an option on a tract of land near the site of his birth. Not on the site, for back in 1886 the solid brick structure of the Bethel Baptist Church (still standing) had preëmpted it. The Bethel Baptists, knowing that Jefferson Davis was a religious man (even if he was a fallen-away Baptist and, since Richmond and the Civil War, a communicant of the more tony Episcopal Church), had originally asked him for the site as a gift. But the land was not in his hands, and now he hadn't the money to buy it back for a gift. Several of the more solvent parishioners bought the land and deeded it, in the name of Jefferson Davis, to the Baptists. The four-room cabin in which his father, Samuel Davis, had nursed his idle dream of breeding race horses before his wife's well-regarded cookery made an inn a practical venture was carefully dismantled, and the components were later reassembled for the Tennessee Centennial of 1897, in Nashville. There the cabin vied for attention, somewhat unsuccessfully, with the newly erected replica of the Parthenon, which proved Nashville to be the "Athens of the South." (The poet Randall Jarrell is reported to have served as the model for the Ganymede on the pediment—a chronological impossibility if we refer to the original structure of 1897, but not if to the permanent reconstruction of the early 1920s.) As for the Bethel Baptist Church, Jefferson Davis paid his last visit to his native state, and county, to attend the dedication of the building, in 1886. He made some rather ecumenical remarks at the dedication, and then he left his gift—a silver Communion service which is preserved there. After the death of Davis, in 1889, the land for the monument, in a tract that was to become "the Park," was bought by the United Confederate Veterans. But it was not until 1917, a few months before the United States embarked on its first great world adventure, that the actual construction of an obelisk of poured concrete was begun.

I was nearly twelve then, and months before, with a pillow at my back to make my scrawny legs reach the pedals, I had begun to drive the family Chevrolet. So, out of my as yet unclarified puzzlement and my confusion of feelings about Jefferson Davis, I drove several times, alone, the miles to the scrubby country of Fairview—then a scattered community, no longer the town of Davisburg or the later Georgetown, as it had been called until it sank back again to the level of a mere settlement. There I might stare at the building shacks and the debris of construction from which rose a gray-white shaft, unsure of my own feelings not merely about Davis (about whom I still knew little) but vaguely, I suppose, about the mystery of the pain, vision, valor, human weakness, and error of the past being somehow transformed into, glorified into, the immobile thrust of concrete (not even the dignity of stone), rising from thistle, mullein, poverty grass, and broken timbers against the blazing blue sky of summer or the paling sky of autumn. By this time, young men, some from the neighborhood, were dying far away across the ocean, but I can't recall that the thought brushed my mind, however fleetingly, that this monument was already antiquated, and that spick-and-span new ones would soon be built to honor blood newly shed.

Was the blank shaft that was rising there trying to say something about that war of long ago when young men had ridden away from the same countryside to die for whatever they had died for? Was the tall shaft, now stubbed at the top, what history was? Certainly these words did not come into my fuddled head. Childhood and adolescence do not live much by words, by abstractions, for words freeze meaning in its living surge, or come only as bubbles that rise and burst from the dark, unpredictable flow of feeling. And, looking back years later, we know how hard it is to sink ourselves again into the old dark wordless flow. We have more and more words now, and being truly adult is largely the effort to make the lying words stand for the old living truth. How often we learn in later life, for instance, that the love we long ago thought we had was a mask for hatred, or hatred a mask for love.

In any case, as I fumble at recollection and try to immerse myself in the dark flow of that moment, it seems that in facing the blank-topped monument I was trying to focus some meaning, however hard to define, on the relation of past and present, old pain and glory and new pain and glory. For I then had only idiotic, infantile envy of those who were grownup enough to go over the ocean toward reality. And the shadow of Jefferson Davis somehow merged with whatever bubble belatedly rose from the dark flow—or it even seemed, now and then, to be part of the dark flow itself.

The next summer, when news of the far-off fighting was the general topic of adult conversation, I went again to Fairview—only once, I think. I did go back in the fall, though, to find that work had stopped. The government had belatedly decided that the monument was not essential to the war effort. For several years, work was suspended. Then, on June 1, 1924, a bronze cap was set on the summit. Certain diehard Confederates, it is said, had wanted to push on to surpass the

Washington Monument, but the common victory in France seemed to make such feeling antiquated, too.

W HO was this Jefferson Davis? Eventually, I came to know something about him, and about the speculations concerning the inner man. In those early days when I visited the unfinished monument, I knew, of course, that he was born in my Todd County—though at the date of his birth, June 3, 1808, the county had not yet been carved from the larger entities of Christian and Logan Counties, now adjacently eastward and westward. Samuel Davis, born of an unsung line of Welsh immigrants who had drifted south from Pennsylvania, entered history by raising a company of frontiersmen in Georgia to take a whack at the redcoats, and then, catching the westward fever, he moved to Kentucky, finally to Christian County, where he settled on six hundred acres of scarcely improved land, built the four-room log structure, and dreamed of raising horses. Whatever limited worldly fortune Samuel had thus far gained, he was a man of philoprogenitive prowess. When a tenth child was born, the father named him Jefferson (for the President) Finis (to set a term to his own obvious talent on corn-shuck or other mattress) Davis (to place him in the line of blood). In the tissue of ironic symbolism that may be read into the later career of the infant, the first two names may be argued to have some unintended significance. With the end of the career of Jefferson Finis Davis came the' end of the dream—already so often debauched—of the author of the Declaration. The new Davis son had long since, perhaps superstitiously, dropped the middle name, probably as early as he was put to his Latin, but who can so easily throw away his fate?

Before the new child was more than a toddler, Samuel had been caught by a new fever: cotton-growing in Missis-sippi. There, somewhat southeast of the town of Natchez, soon to be the glamorous capital of King Cotton, he came in for modest prosperity, hav-ing got in on the cotton boom early enough to acquire slaves, even if never to hold a great plantation with the mandatory Greek columns. But one of his older sons—Joseph Davis, twen-

27

ty-three years older than little Jeff—
who had become a successful lawyer,
did have a great plantation, Hurricane,
and this older brother, bit by bit, assumed the paternal role and defined
the character and aspirations of the boy.

Less than a year after little Jeff's
birth—before he could have character or aspirations worth mentioning, of
course—another man-child was born,
some hundred miles away in Kentucky, in another log cabin, to even
poorer parentage. The parents of
Abraham Lincoln were somewhat
ambitionlessly caught up in a drift
northward, across the Ohio and into
frontier country, where, in spite of
poverty and hardship, the boy, driven
by some remorseless will to excel,
reached out for learning and for a
place in the world of power which
would be worthy of the self he felt he
was. By early middle age, the boy born
in the frontier cabin was a success, living in a spacious white house in town,
practicing law for good fees, and dab-
bling in politics. Lincoln was also a
man of remarkable physical strength—
a strength that was to sustain him in
the strenuous years between 1861 and
1865, while Davis, not far away, in

Richmond, was being tortured by ill health, sleeplessness, and neuralgia. What would have happened if Thomas Lincoln had followed the drive to Mississippi as the land where energy and cunning in a new fluidity might make a man great—the same land that William Faulkner's great-grandfather came to as a penniless youth and that Faulkner himself was to write about? Or what would have happened if Samuel Davis had sought his luck northward across the Ohio? How much is a man the product of his society?

In any case, Joseph Davis—now an aristocrat and a "cotton snob"—sent his youngest brother up to a famous Catholic monastic school in Kentucky, where, at the age of about seven, he might begin the education of a gentleman, and where he precociously decided that he wanted to become a Catholic. His request to adopt that faith was refused as premature, and a kindly father offered him a sandwich of good Catholic cheese in consolation, but there he may have absorbed the germ of rigid logic that later marked his mind and his views of history, law, and politics. This, however, is speculation. Another piece of speculation: the man who conducted the party to Kentucky was a Major Hinds, a friend and old companion-in-arms of Andrew Jackson, and on the way north the party spent some time at the Hermitage, near Nashville. There the boy saw his first "great man." Young Jeff had actually seen the human image of greatness.

Later, after Jeff had returned to Mississippi and had spent a few years in local schools there, Joseph sent him back to Kentucky—to Transylvania University, at Lexington, an institution that was then renowned as one of the best universities in the country. There the young Davis pursued his study of the classics. But this was interrupted by an appointment to West Point, a training ground for greatness. The document of appointment was signed by none other than John C. Calhoun, the Secretary of War, and thus Davis was first linked with the statesman whose mantle as the premier champion of states' rights he eventually assumed. But once at West Point the young man was associating with many to whom his fate would be linked, whom he would know as commanders of friend or foe—a few of whom wearing Confederate gray were not to see eye to eye with their President.

As for Davis himself, he was no Robert E. Lee—for Lee was the perfect cadet, already moving in the subtle aura of greatness. It is hard, in looking at later photographs of the tall, hollow-cheeked man whose face twitched with neuralgia and whose left eye was bleared in blindness, to remember that the young Davis was vigorous, agile, poetically handsome, high-spirited, somewhat rebellious, given to off-grounds carousing and eggnog parties, and liberally decorated with demerits. And later, at an Indian outpost, now with a lieutenant's commission, the irrepressible young man—this according to the report of a Potawatomi Indian chief presumably present—seized an extraordinarily handsome young squaw, who was respectably dancing a quadrille, and converted the dance into a waltz so that he might slip an arm around her lissomeness. Then, in his excitement, he detached himself from the charmer to dance alone, to "jerk and wiggle" and leap and yell like an Indian. Eggnog, firewater, concupiscence of the flesh, or manly high spirits—whatever it was—might well have led to a bloody affray, for the young

31

squaw's brother, sensing insult, came at him, scalping knife against pistol. But the commanding colonel, who had just been laughing at the lieutenant's antics, intervened.

Such a young Davis did in truth exist—a cadet who graduated twenty-third in a class of thirty-three. And these are not the only glimpses we catch of him, for he was on active duty in 1832, during the Black Hawk War, on the old Northwest Frontier in Illinois and Wisconsin. It was a war of which he was fair-minded enough to report that the only heroes were the Indians, and that if one action (that of holding off pursuing troopers while a river could be crossed) had been "performed by white men" it "would have been immortalized." He himself carried out his military duties well enough to be given, after the somewhat shabby victory at Bad Axe River—little more than a massacre—the honor of having in his personal charge Chief Black Hawk and other captives. Black Hawk, in a dictated narrative, referred to his captor as "a good and brave young chief, with whose conduct I was much pleased"—at least when Davis saved him and his warriors from the japes of gaping crowds. But at St. Louis Davis turned his charge over to Brigadier General Henry Atkinson. Acting under orders to take strictest measures to guard the prisoners, Atkinson saw to it that irons were put on. One cannot but wonder if the image of the manacled Black Hawk, who had long ago said that "a brave war chief would prefer death to dishonor," flashed before the mind of Davis when he, old, sick, and defeated, struggled as his captors applied the outrage of superfluous shackles.

While Davis was doing his Indian fighting, another name known to the record was that of a young elected captain of a company of raw recruits being mustered in—a captain who was years later described on hearsay by Varina Davis in her memoirs as "a tall, gawky, slab-sided, homely, young man." This was Abraham Lincoln, and, again according to Mrs. Davis, one of the two lieutenants administering the oath to the captain and his men (these were conscripts, according to the historian A. J. Beveridge) later became the Major Robert Anderson "who fired the first gun at Fort Sumter," and the other was, "in after years, the

President of the Confederate States." Of course, in relation to Anderson the use of the words "first" and "at" is deceptive, for Anderson fired *from* the fort *against* the attack from shore batteries. Defective proof further impairs the anecdote, and Mrs. Davis admits in her text that her husband remembered swearing in the recruits but not Lincoln. Of the Black Hawk War, Lincoln said only, "I fought, bled, and came away." But the bleeding, he added, with characteristic humorous understatement, was "from bloody struggles with mosquitoes."

Whatever the full truth, the thread of irony, and of pathos as well, runs through the event. Encounters, friendships, family blood were the woof of which the Civil War was the warp. For instance, Simon Bolivar Buckner, the friend of Ulysses S. Grant at West Point who later encountered him on the street in New York, nearly a drunken wreck, and paid his board bill and other debts and gave him encouragement, was to become the Confederate general who officially surrendered to Grant at Fort Donelson—where Grant, superfluously, offered him his private purse. And when Grant, after his disgraceful Presidency, struggling to rehabilitate himself and leave his family something by writing his memoirs, was, at the end, dying of cancer, it was the same old friend, Simon Bolivar Buckner, now with a thriving career and a young bride, who came to make, after all those years, a last, private visit. When, a day later, he emerged to face the congregated reporters, to their importunities he gave little satisfaction.

In the years before these friendships were broken or sealed, and familial blood was shed, young Davis fell in love with the sixteen-year-old daughter of the officer in command of his frontier post, Colonel Zachary Taylor. The young girl had an eye for the handsome young officer with the deep, poetic glance, but the father offered objections, the official one being that he did not want his daughter married to a military man. If the record of the Potawatomi chief is accurate, however, Colonel Taylor had also seen the squaw episode, and he may not have wanted such high spirits in the family. But Sarah Knox Taylor, usually called Knox, had a mind and heart of her own, and on June 17, 1835, with her father absent from the ceremony, she was married to her lieutenant at the house of an aunt in Kentucky.

She was not, however, marrying a military man. Brother Joseph had given Jefferson a plantation—Brierfield—adjoining his own Hurricane, and had given him credit on generous terms, enabling him to buy fourteen slaves. So the lieutenant was now a planter, even if his house was far from imposing and much of his land was yet to be brought under cultivation. The idyll at Brierfield was short. By fall, both bride and bridegroom were down with a virulent fever. The gift from the generous Joseph had been a gift of death—and perhaps, as it turned out, a gift of destiny. By September, at Locust Grove plantation, in Louisiana, where one of Jefferson's sisters lived, both bride and bridegroom were at the point of death, neither knowing of the serious plight of the other. One night, the bridegroom, waking from his stupor, heard the distant sound of the bride's voice singing "Fairy Bells," a song of their courtship. He struggled toward the voice, but by the time he reached her room she had passed from her delirium into a last coma. The stubborn little Knox had had her will and her love, and this was what had come of it.

One thing that may have come of it was to make Jefferson Davis great. Shaken in soul and body, he sought recovery in Cuba, then distraction in New York and Washington. The great world, however, was not for him now. To reclaim Brierfield was a passion and an anodyne. There was another anodyne. No longer the high-spirited youth who had accumulated demerits at West Point, Davis filled his lonely evenings with grinding study of great literature: Shakespeare, certainly; and the English Romantic poets and eighteenth-century prose, barbed or eloquent. He read history and the works of such theorists as John Locke and Adam Smith. He sank himself word by word into the literature of our national origins, of the philosophers and the politicians. He practically memorized the Constitution. Nor did he forget the classics.

The new emptiness of the house at Brierfield was too much for him now. He spent much of his time at Hurricane, and there, with Joseph, he found the clash of minds and interests, collaboration in ideas, and a never-ending tide of speculation. There, too, he found new books, for Joseph was reputed to own the finest library in the state. So Joseph added his services as tutor to his already numerous benefactions.

Undoubtedly, the pure pleasure of intellectual adventure was involved in the relationship, but both Joseph and Jefferson had proved themselves as men of action, too. Joseph had cut a figure as a lawyer and a planter. As for Jefferson, in addition to the ordinary military career, he had seriously considered challenging his commanding colonel to a duel, feeling that the colonel's opposition to the marriage with Knox amounted to an affront to honor. But the challenge was never given; the young lieutenant must have finally realized that this was a peculiar way to carry on a courtship. (Later, Davis challenged a fellow-senator in deadly earnest, and only the interposition of friends prevented the encounter.) The impulse to action may well have lain latent behind those evening hours of study or debate. Times had been changing. John C. Calhoun, for instance, had long since fathered the doctrine of nullification in South Carolina. (As it happened, though, secession had previously been a popular sentiment in New England, and on the verge of the Civil War it reappeared in the Northeast.) Southern Whiggery had been based on the sense of a solidarity of interests among moneyed men of whatever section, but now it was beginning to wither on the local vine, for planters were becoming aware, tardily, of what the tariff question held for them. The North was more and more committed to manufacturing, and wanted high tariffs on imports of competing goods to maintain the domestic price; the South, with a mainly extractive economy, wanted to buy manufactured goods cheap, and therefore favored low tariffs. In addition to this split, that in regard to slavery was increasing. There had been considerable emancipation sentiment in the South, and even emancipation societies. Emancipation barely missed in the Virginia Legislature in 1830–31, but new events, some economic, and some more complex— Nat Turner's Rebellion, rebellion in the West Indies, the rise of frenetic Garrisonian abolitionism—gave new tensions to the slavery question, and emancipation sentiment in the South receded.

Jefferson Davis, like many Southerners of the early era, had been a somewhat unself-conscious Southerner, a wanderer in many states, with a grave oath taken long back to affirm a national loyalty. Besides, the South he had been born in lay far to the north of Mississippi. Now, however, Davis, the wanderer, was becoming a Mississippian. He was being "Southernized" not only by association and study but by occupation: he was a planter and a slavemaster. Even so, the kind of slavemaster he was set him apart from many others. Apparently, he did not conceive of slavery as an eternal institution justified by the Holy Writ—or did not conceive of it that way consistently. With no date of emancipation perceptible in the drift of history, he did organize Brierfield for a kind of training that would help protect the black man, once freed, from being exploited by ruthless white competition. This is not to say that Davis—any more than Lincoln, a number of abolitionists, and a large majority of the white population—believed that the black man and the white were equally endowed. But he did believe, within undefined limits, in educability and progress for the black.

The overseer of Brierfield was an extremely efficient black man who had been with Davis since early in his military career and whose intelligence and sense of duty were never doubted. At Brierfield, too, work was assigned according to capacity and taste. Festivals like marriages, births, and Christmas were provided for, and so were rituals of grief. Careful attention to health (including regular dental service) was maintained. Free time was allowed for personal projects for profit, such as gardening, animal raising, crafts, and storekeeping, with the master's household and, presumably, others as customers. Discipline and decency were maintained by requiring appearance before a jury of blacks with a black judge, and there was cross-examination of witnesses. Punishment was set by the court and administered by blacks. The master reserved one right: to reduce a sentence. In other words, Davis was the type of slaveholder that to the true-blue abolitionist was the deepest-dyed villain: the master who tried to treat his slaves decently tended to make slavery acceptable both to the slave and to the moral sensibilities of the general Northern public. A man like Davis, whatever his deepest unconscious motives, struck at one of the cherished notions of the hard-core abolitionist—the cherished doctrine that the South was one great brothel and the slave-holder a racist fiend who chuckled before he quaffed his wine from a bowl that had lately been the skull of a black man. (Even the gentle John Greenleaf Whittier, in the poem "Amy Wentworth," accepted this useful myth.)

Selfish though his unconscious motives may have been, Davis realized that emancipation as such worked no magic—something that is clear from this morning's newspaper and will be from tomorrow's. Lincoln, the signer of the Emancipation Proclamation, was also perfectly aware of this. When asked, toward the end of the Civil War, what the ex-slave would do, he replied, "Root"—an echo of the old saying "Root, hog, or die." It is a pity that we cannot know the expression on Lincoln's face and in his voice—cynical detachment or outraged sarcasm—as he uttered the all too astute prediction.

But history rolled on in its tragic way, though one thing along that way was not tragic. Joseph, as watchful as ever, invited a marriageable young lady named Varina Howell to visit Hurricane. Half his brother's age, she had had a good classical education; had raven-black hair, a cream complexion, and the most lithe and graspable of waists, in an age that greatly admired such a thing in a nubile female; and was charming and well connected. In a letter to her mother after first laying eyes on Jefferson Davis, she wrote that she couldn't tell whether he was young or old (he was thirty-five, and the nearly fatal fever had left his cheeks somewhat gaunt); and she observed a certain dogmatism in his opinions. How shrewdly the girl half his age summed him up! She thought him to be "the kind of person I should expect to rescue one from a mad dog at any risk, but to insist upon a stoical indifference to the fright afterward." She wound up, rather ambiguously: "Would you believe it, he is refined and cultivated and yet he is a Democrat." But she had already noted that he had "a peculiarly sweet voice and a winning manner of asserting himself." This blossom, whose accent in Latin both Joseph and Jefferson admired, came from Natchez, where, with wealth, Whiggery still reigned, and to indicate her political preference she wore a cameo brooch exhibiting a strongbox, undoubtedly full of money, and a great beast of a dog couchant to guard it. But the "peculiarly sweet voice" did its work, and one day the brooch wasn't worn. Politics was not to make strife, however muted, in bed-chamber or at breakfast table.

Davis soon went to Congress, where he quickly proclaimed the doctrine of states' rights and offered a resolution that, though it was then shelved, seems fatefully prophetic of the first shell to burst over Fort Sumter—a resolution that state troops should replace national troops in all federal forts situated within the bounds of a state.

The new congressman quickly relinquished mere talk for an active hand in promoting another cause dear to the Southern heart—the extension of the country's frontiers to the west and south. Not that expansionism and the doctrine of Manifest Destiny were limited to the South. The flood of immigration to the Oregon country and the near-war with Great Britain were not the work of "the slavocracy." John Jacob Astor and his fur company were not slaveholders, nor was John Quincy Adams, who proclaimed that it was the American duty to make "the [Oregon] wilderness blossom as the rose . . . and subdue the earth, which we are commanded to do by the first behest of God Almighty." In other words, neither South nor North had much concern with the ethics of conquest. The two merely had a private quarrel about the disposition of spoils.

The Mexican War came. Davis resigned from Congress and accepted a colonel's commission from the State of Mississippi as commander of the regiment of Mississippi Rifles—a volunteer organization, which was armed with a new percussion rifle, and to which he gave the spit and polish and cutting edge of West Point. The regiment served under the command of General Zachary Taylor, Old Rough and Ready, who years before had briefly been the recalcitrant father-in-law of Davis. The war Davis had was a fighting war, and he did well at it: well at Monterrey and famously at

Buena Vista, where, at a crucial point in the battle, his Rifles received the powerful charge of Santa Anna's lancers—red jackets and wind-whipped pennons—that was supposed to give the coup de grâce. But Davis received the charge at the upper end of a gorge, his troops in a V-shaped disposition with the lower end open to the assault, and the V became a death trap as the lancers piled into it—against riflemen they could not well reach, who were marksmen from a state where a bad marksman was almost as difficult to find as a hen's tooth.

Davis even had the glory of a wound—in the foot, with blood welling in the boot as he continued to command; and later he had crutches on ceremonial occasions when he was received as a hero. It is reported, though not on incontrovertible authority, that after Buena Vista Old Rough and Ready grasped the hand of the hero and declared that his poor dead daughter had been a better judge of a man than he himself had been. Other honors are, however, beyond dispute. President James Polk raised him to the rank of brigadier general of volunteers, only to have the document decorously thrown back into his face with a lesson in constitutionality: no one but the governor of Mississippi could legally promote a colonel of the Mississippi Rifles.

Davis heard himself toasted as "the Game Cock of the South," and as such he was soon appointed senator. But the game of politics he had not learned (and never did learn): the deal; the nature of combinations; easy fellowship; compromise; the slipperiness of logic; humor; patience; generosity; the ready smile. His weapon was forged of his learning, his devotion to principle, his frigid dignity, his reputation for heroism and honor, and, most of all, his logic—cold, abstract, and sometimes inhuman. He would have been incapable of grasping what Justice Oliver Wendell Holmes had in mind when, years later, he said, "The life of law has not been logic: it has been experience." And the incapacity of grasping such an idea was the tragic flaw in the midst of the hero's multifarious endowments.

In however ironical a way, time was on the side of Davis. Though he was defeated when he left the Senate to run for the governorship of Mississippi—and defeated as a secessionist—the application of "squatter sovereignty" to the territories and to "Bleeding Kansas" waited just over the temporal horizon. Meanwhile, Davis was snatched from his cotton planting to become Secretary of War under the new President, Franklin Pierce—a role that even unforgiving enemies had to admit he performed with brilliance (and with ingenuity, suggesting that camel corps be established to handle the Indians of the arid Southwest and improve communication with California). Strangely, his labors as Secretary of War were undertaken for the Union. Had Davis, after reading the political temperature of Mississippi in his defeat as an immediate secessionist, modified his doctrine of states' rights?

No. Davis was still a Southerner, and presumably hoped that he could exercise power best in the framework of the Union. Even after he returned to Mississippi, just on the eve of the Civil War, as a leading exponent of Southern rights, he found it hard to face the logically ultimate step of secession. Only with the disintegration of the old Democratic Party, the election of Lincoln, and the secession of South

Carolina did Davis accept the conclusion—accept it as expedient, that is, for he had never doubted its constitutionality. In departing from the Senate (to which he had been elected after his stint as Secretary of War), he made himself amply clear: "If I thought that Mississippi was acting without sufficient provocation . . . I should still . . . because of my allegiance to the State of which I am a citizen, have been bound by her action." Many men, most notably Robert E. Lee, staked their lives and their sacred honor on this point. How odd it all seems now—when the sky hums with traffic, and eight-lane highways stinking of high-test rip across hypothetical state lines, and half the citizens don't know or care where they were born just so they can get somewhere fast.

IN any case, Davis had come a long way from Fairview, Todd County, Kentucky. On February 10, 1861, he was standing by his wife in a rose garden at Brierfield, where they had been pruning bushes. A telegram informed him that by the convention called in Montgomery, Alabama, he had been unanimously elected President of the

Provisional Government of the Confederacy. On the evening of February 17th, under the light of torches, amid a great crowd, an old-time fire-eater, William Yancey, announced, "The man and the hour have met!" Davis would have preferred the commission of a general. The memory of the famous V formation and the victory at Buena Vista remained with him.

What kind of President was Davis? It is hard to answer that question, for it evokes multitudinous considerations, most of which doubtless never crossed the mind of the old man under the cedar tree, meditating on the past while an ignorant little boy sat there tailor-fashion on the ground. Some historians will sum the matter up by saying that if Lincoln had been at Richmond and Davis at Washington the South would have been free. That is, in spite of the many advantages the North enjoyed, Lincoln would have been as head of the Confederacy a crucial factor, and in the South could have psychologically molded a national spirit out of the paradox of states' rights, which, of course, naturally denied the possibility of nationalism. But this is the wildest of ifs.

The new President of the Confederacy was no longer the young-old man of beautiful manners and the poetic glance noted by Varina Howell in her letter to her mother. Nor was he the decisive colonel, not yet forty, who had sprung the lethal trap at Buena Vista. He was now past fifty, erect but even more gaunt-cheeked, blind in one eye, racked by murderous neuralgia, certainly neurotic in some undiagnosable way (perhaps suffering from an inner struggle of values), given to irritability that could break through his iron mask of will. Though he was capable of tact (sometimes tact in the face of severe provocation), and even of occasional humor, he lacked the indefinable sense for "handling" men, the intuitive understanding of others, and, ultimately, perhaps, self-confidence. He was incapable of catching the public imagination. He could sometimes inspire devotion, but his enclosed personality sometimes made him seem "cold as a lizard," as Sam Houston put it. Houston also called him as "ambitious as Lucifer." Set a thief to catch a thief! Ambitious, with little doubt, Davis was, but in no such simple, though cunning, way as Houston himself.

There are many kinds of ambition, ranging from the trivial vanity of strut and preen, with no relation to accomplishment, to that fuelling, depersonalizing devotion to an objective endeavor, the locale of which may be a poet's desk or a soldier's battlefield. And what are we to say about Lincoln, whose ambition, according to William Herndon, his law partner and intimate, "was a little engine that knew no rest," and who, Herndon also said, "had an idea that he was equal to, if not superior to, all things"? We can say that Lincoln's engine of ambition was drawn into a complex of depersonalizing values. And what of the ambition of that ambiguous hero of liberalism Justice Holmes? What are we to make of the letter of William James (to Henry) analyzing the character of that old friend of his youth—it was later that he became Justice—and describing him as "a powerful battery, formed like a planing machine to gouge a deep and self-beneficial groove through life"? In any case, not simple ambition or the desire for a self-beneficial groove through life, any more than naked energy, maintained Davis for the four gruelling years. Iron will, self-denial, self-discipline, devotion to principle were certainly there—and, it may be safely hazarded, his conception of honor. But we can ultimately only guess about Davis. The historian who called him the Sphinx of the Confederacy was right.

There is, however, the simple fact of age and health. Though Lincoln was less than a year younger than Davis, his extraordinary physical strength and his health—no doubt conserved, in spite of his own dark moments of spirit, by patience, humor, and self-confidence—made him seem a generation younger. And this fact reminds one of another, more demonstrable fact. Grant was some fifteen years younger than Lee, and the significance of this fact has been emphasized by historians, who have compared the number of days lost from indisposition by the two commanders. In fact, during most of the war Lee was suffering from heart trouble, diagnosed as rheumatism until his death. As for Sherman, he was forty-one when the war began.

From the beginning, the North enjoyed obvious advantages, and Davis had to struggle against them. The disparity in population was tremendous; in addition, the North could draw on an almost inexhaustible reservoir of foreign recruits. At the very beginning of the war, General Winfield Scott had formulated the throttling "Anaconda" plan, which underlay later strategy, since a superior, more flexible military organization, allowing for variation and modification, could basically retain it. Although the largely improvised Confederate Navy and privateers did vast damage to Northern shipping, the control of inland waterways by gunboat, the capture of Southern ports, and the embargo, however imperfect, gave the North a tremendous edge. Agriculture in the North was already somewhat mechanized and was directed to food production. General education in the North was much superior, there was much greater acquaintance with mechanics, and business organization was more highly developed, as was the industrial plant. In 1864, in his annual message to Congress, Lincoln summed up the increased prosperity brought to the North by the Civil War: "It is of noteworthy interest that the steady expansion of population, improvement, and governmental institutions over the new and unoccupied portion of our country have scarcely been checked . . . that we have *more* men *now* than we had when the war *began;* that we are not exhausted, nor in process of exhaustion; that we are *gaining* strength. . . . Material resources are now more complete and abundant than ever." He mentioned, in passing, the construction of the Pacific railroad and the increasing exploitation of gold, silver, and mercury in the West. In other words, the North was getting richer from the war. Another important factor working for Lincoln was that in spite of his avowed racism (which may have contributed to his general popularity) he knew how to exploit the superior moral position of emancipation. And, most important, Lincoln, in the words of Alexander H. Stephens, the Vice-President of the Confederacy, raised the idea of the Union "to the sublimity of religious mysticism"—and managed to make himself the recognized embodiment of that mysticism.

The main idea that Davis was officially committed to defend (however much he may have vacillated on the issue for reasons of expediency) was the doctrine of states' rights. But this doctrine involved a suicidal paradox. In "Why the North Won the Civil War," Richard N. Current writes, "A Confederacy formed by particularist politicians could hardly be expected to adopt promptly those centralist policies... which victory demanded." The crucial doctrine left no way for Davis—certainly for a man of his temperament—to deal with such governors as Joseph Emerson Brown, of Georgia, and Zebulon Baird Vance, of North Carolina, who, for all practical purposes, were doctrinaire to the point of mania or treason in withholding men and supplies from the central government. In fact, as the first Confederate Secretary of War, Leroy Pope Walker, pointed out, in the early days of the war two hundred thousand volunteers could not be armed, because the doctrine of states' rights allowed individual states to withhold equipment. Frank L. Owsley, in "State Rights in the Confederacy," summed up the paradox when he wrote that the epitaph on the tombstone of the incipient nation should have read "Died of State Rights."

Davis and the South also faced other

problems involving paradox. The great Confederate hope for recognition abroad lay in the power of King Cotton. The South assumed that British mills had to have cotton, and Yankee shipping as well as Yankee mills had to have it. But the gamble on cotton backfired. France was sympathetic but would not act without England. The British, though they were divided in their sympathies (with even the liberal Gladstone at one time, ironically, sympathetic to the Confederate cause), quickly found that the war was God's blessing to them. First, there was no immediate pressure on them, because they had a good store of cotton on hand, and soon there began to be cotton from India. Second, the seas were being swept of their great rival, the large and expertly designed American merchant marine (the Confederate privateers and their effects on shipping-insurance rates ably abetting Divine Providence). Third, the munitions business—the British dealt with both sides—was a true bonanza. There was indeed strong sentiment against slavery, but the British millworkers' love of freedom has apparently been overadvertised, and many a millworker would apparently swell a demonstration on one side one day (for a fee, of course) and swell an opposing one the next day—grayback or Yankee, who cared. Anyway, the millworker could not vote, and those who ran the country were in no mood to strangle their own prosperity. Besides, if the Confederacy should be recognized, war with the United States would be almost inevitable (Lincoln and William Henry Seward, his Secretary of State, could be very tough in their dealings with the Court of St. James's), and Canada might well be lost.

It is true that in France as well as in England there was strong sentiment against slavery, but when the idea of offering emancipation as a bribe for recognition was finally beginning to be put forward in the Confederacy it was too late to be of any use, besides striking paradoxically at a necessary, if not sufficient, reason for the war: slavery. And a parallel instance appeared when the idea of enlisting blacks for Confederate armies (with the implied promise of freedom) was successfully brought forward—a paradox best formulated by the politician Howell Cobb, of Georgia, who opposed the idea: "If slaves will make good soldiers, our whole theory of slavery is wrong." Actually, some blacks were enlisted and wore the gray, but only toward the end of the war.

So, with states' rights obviously bringing on disaster, King Cotton dethroned, and blacks wearing Confederate gray, little was left of the ideas that had made the Confederacy—only secession, in fact. But with the armies of Sherman and Grant closing in and defeatism stalking the land, what would become of that notion—a notion that for many eminent Southerners, including Davis and Lee, had been from the first dubious or rueful? Merely some notion of Southern identity remained, however hazy or fuddled; it was not until after Appomattox that the conception of Southern identity truly bloomed—a mystical conception, vague but bright, floating high beyond the criticism of brutal circumstances.

WHAT should Davis have done? He might have insisted on a military reorganization to remedy the cumbersomeness of the departmental system, under which large-scale flexible planning was not readily feasible. Perhaps some action might have been taken—in the face of intransigent Southern personalities and principles—to connect the fatally unconnected rail systems (some even had different gauges of rails), in order to exploit the geographical advantage of interior lines and to distribute food and military supplies where they were needed instead of letting rifles rust and food rot. Perhaps more attention to internal problems, to questions of finance, and, more important, to morale. Perhaps, even with the departmental system, more attention to the crucial West, especially to Vicksburg. Perhaps less favoritism, especially to West Point commanders. Perhaps a change in the conscription law that made the owner of twenty slaves exempt from military service—a change that would at least have defanged the poisonous witticism that the bloodshed was "a rich man's war and a pore man's fight." Perhaps a capital farther away than Richmond from the frontier (Montgomery, say), to free Southern forces for maneuver. Perhaps the risk of a pursuit into Washington itself on the heels of an army in panic and total disorder after the First Battle of Manassas. In any case, an abandonment of the policy of maintaining a defensive posture and waiting for European recognition, and an assumption of greater and more immediate military initiative—as Robert Toombs, Secretary of State of the Confederacy in 1861, and later a brigadier general, had urged from the beginning. But each of these proposals presented difficulties.

Davis was what he was, and he was caught in the complications of the world he lived in—a world in which virtues could sometimes turn into liabilities. One way to approach the question of the suitability of Davis as a war President is to ask who among those available in 1861 would have made a better President.

By and large, underlying many of the particular problems were fundamental difficulties built into the very nature of the Confederacy. It can even be argued that the factor underlying all other factors was a state of mind that existed in the North but not in the South. Though the Northern philosophy was unformulated, we can recognize it in the context of thought that led William James, in the end, to his doctrine of pragmatism. This was the state of mind that saw history not in terms of abstract, fixed principles but as a wavering flow of shifting values and contingencies, each to be confronted on the terms of its context. Both Calhoun and Davis (with thousands of others) saw the Constitution as equivalent to the tablets that Moses delivered from Sinai, in contrast to Lincoln, who apparently regarded it in some such evolutionary sense as that of Justice Holmes when Holmes wrote of the development of law.

This Northern bias toward experience was definitely related to the successful conduct of the war. To begin with, once Lincoln had passed the early period of inaction he had no compunction about brushing aside legal technicalities. Without a shadow of legal justification, he had hordes of Northern citizens seized on the merest suspicion, or the slightest and most prejudiced hearsay, and held them incommunicado, ignoring the right of habeas corpus and the Supreme Court. In the same spirit, he ordered telegraph offices raided en masse for copies of messages, and, with no shadow of legal authority, he reached into the Treasury for what sums he deemed requisite. Lincoln did make a sort of bow to the Constitution by implying that in violating it he was saving it. (It may be recalled that early in life he had replaced the Deity with his own notion of evolution in nature and man.) Lincoln had proclaimed, at Cooper Union, on February 27, 1860, that "right makes might," and certainly, except in his darkest and most skeptical meditations, he would not have agreed with Justice Holmes's pragmatic avowal that the "good" is what results from *"force majeure,"* and that every society "rests on the death of men." But he obviously did believe that society could rest on the illegal jailing of men', and that law and the Constitution depended ultimately on need, preference, and cold-blooded power.

More than a contrast between Lincoln and Davis is involved. The contrast lay in the two societies—one embracing antique values, the other in the process of developing new ones. To take a small but symbolic military matter, the Confederate notion of leadership was to lead—personally. At Gettysburg, for instance, Brigadier General William Barksdale swept over the battery at the Peach Orchard well ahead of his men, and—hatless, white hair flying, sword pointing up Cemetery Ridge—continued to lead until his conspicuous valor invited a Union officer to detail a whole company of riflemen to get that man. Forrest is not a perfect example, for he rose from private to general, but, *main à main*, he slew twenty-nine adversaries in his lifetime and had thirty horses shot from under him—three at Fort Pillow alone. This is not to say that when occasion demanded, Federal officers, too, did not coolly expose themselves to enemy fire—Grant, for example, at Vicksburg—but the code was very different. The outmoded chivalric gesture, according to Douglas Southall Freeman's analysis, seriously reduced the numbers of the Confederate officer corps.

An even more fundamental contrast between the antagonists lay in their views of the nature of war. It is true that at the beginning men of influence on both sides tended to accept the old-fashioned notion of chivalric war. At Fort Sumter, throngs of Southern onlookers cheered when, after a pause that suggested surrender, Robert Anderson's defending guns again answered the overwhelming bombardment; and when surrender finally occurred Anderson was presented with the shot-torn flag as a trophy—which he said he would treasure to become his shroud. And when the boat brought him from Sumter to the dock, the Southern spectators received him with the respect due a hero. Another instance, more theoretical, appears in General George B. McClellan's early statement that his philosophy forbade war on civilians and the confiscation of property. When General George Gordon Meade—long before he was victor at Gettysburg—was ordered to seize the property of a Confederate sympathizer, he held that the North should behave like "the afflicted parent who is compelled to chasten his erring child and who performs his duty with a sad heart." And, later, the gallant young Colonel Robert Gould Shaw—who eventually died vainly leading his black regiment up the shifting sands on the slopes of Fort Wagner, at Charleston—wrote his wife that if he should be executed for insubordination it would be because he could not again follow such an order as he had recently followed: to destroy "the unoffending little town of Darien, Georgia."

But General Quincy Gillmore, unable to subdue the forts at Charleston, was moved by no such chivalry. One of the new breed, he set up a great gun in the swamps outside the city—the Swamp Angel, it was called, and its name became the title of a poem by Melville—which, with shells of the fiercely inflammatory Greek fire, carried war to the civilian population. It was just as well for Colonel Shaw that the duty had not been assigned to him.

Sherman is, of course, the most widely advertised of the new men— the inventors of total war. In the beginning, he was not "modern," but he ruthlessly followed the logic of experience to the concept that we now accept as normal. The enemy is not only a "hostile army" but a "hostile people." Terror, Sherman said, is a "weapon," and "war is not popularity-seeking." There is a straight line of logic leading from Sherman's theory to Coventry, buzz bombs on London, the Dresden fire raid, the Tokyo fire raid, and Hiroshima. War was hell, and Sherman strove to make it so, but once the logical end was accomplished he could write that the suffering of the South was "beyond comprehension."

As for Grant, he was a modern man, too, and not only in his later worship of wealth, fat cigars, and big businessmen. Though he flinched from the sight of blood and could eat only overdone meat (and then only the meat of large animals), he learned to become "Grant the butcher." Once face to face with Lee, unconquerable at the chessboard of war, he fought a war of swap-out, knowing that only the balance sheet of blood could insure victory. He had an incalculable amount of blood to swap. And, to make certain that the swap system worked to the utmost, he refused after a battle any truce for the burial of the dead and the succor of the wounded. By the same token, he refused exchanges of prisoners; his theory was that a man could as well serve his country starving in Andersonville as standing in the battle line. Unremitting pressure, at any cost, was the policy of a man who loathed the sight of blood but had come face to face with reality. He was purely logical, and after the war he stated the theory he had developed: "The art of war is simple enough. Find out where your enemy is. Get at him as soon as you can. Strike him as hard as you can, and keep moving." A perfect theory, if you can pay what the then soldier (later Justice) Holmes called, in a letter to his father, "the butcher's bill." And there was one more factor, of a different order, that made Grant a "modern" man in his military attitude: as T. Harry Williams has pointed out, Grant developed the relationship between military thinking and political thinking. He and Lincoln understood each other.

Poor Davis—he was not a modern man in any sense of the word but a conservative called to manage what was, in one sense, a revolution. Honor, perhaps, more than victory, was, in the midst of ill fortune, ineptitudes, and even stupidities, his guiding star, as it may have been that of Lee, Richard Taylor, and others who, though they may never have believed in victory, put their state loyalty first.

WARS tend to be iffy. And there were undoubtedly ifs in the Civil War—historians are still engaged with them. But the modern men won, and from that moment all the ifs disappeared. Toward midnight on April 2, 1865, Davis and his government abandoned Richmond to flee southward. Lincoln came upriver to view the blackened ruins of Richmond. Senator Charles Sumner, of Massachusetts, who was with a second party of Union dignitaries, appropriated the ivory gavel of the Confederate Senate. Returning to Washington, in a distinguished company that included the Marquis de Chambrun, Lincoln could see from shipboard the birthplace of Washington and of Lee—a symbolic panorama of the old nation that had died in 1861—and then felt an impulse to read Shakespeare to the party and to himself. Thus occurred the unforgettable moment that seemed to sum up his earlier succession of direfully predictive dreams in one passage:

> Duncan is in his grave;
> After life's fitful fever he sleeps well. . . .

He read on, to the end:

> Nothing
> Can touch him further.

He paused, and then repeated the passage. The ensuing silence was broken by his wife, who seems to have had an inimitable gift for the irrelevant. She firmly declared that Jefferson Davis ought to be hanged. Lincoln replied, "Judge not that ye be not judged"—a remark that he had earlier had occasion to make to the same statement, from another trivially patriotic mouth, and was to make again.

Appomattox came. Lincoln had a recurrence of an old dream of being on a strange kind of vessel floating to a mystic shore, and recounted it to Gideon Welles, the Secretary of the Navy—presumably because he was handy, not simply because it fell into his department. Lincoln attended "Our American Cousin" at Ford's Theatre and finally reached the mystic shore, dying on April 15th, and leaving Vice-President Andrew Johnson, his successor, full of gall from his deprived childhood and hatred of the likes of Davis, to put a reward of a hundred thousand dollars on the head of the Confederate President as accessory to murder.

Davis, with fewer and fewer com-

70

panions, continued his flight. Heading
west to cross the Mississippi and con-
tinue the war from Texas, his little
party stopped for the night in South
Georgia, where, near Irwinville, on
May 10, 1865, they were captured by
a hog-lucky detachment of federal cavalry. And there, with Davis wearing a
shawl that his wife had thrown about
his shoulders, began the myth that
he had tried to escape in women's
clothes—an episode that, staged as a
comic skit, was to enrich P. T. Barnum and flatter the hearts of patriots.
Barnum omitted the looting of the
Davis baggage by heroes hunting for
the remains of the Confederate Treasury which Davis was supposed to have
made off with, and the sight of troopers in blue gobbling the meagre breakfast prepared for the Davis children.
Davis is reported to have said to the
colonel who had taken him, "The
worst of all is that I should be captured by a band of thieves and scoundrels." Though they found no treasure, the thieves and scoundrels were
now prosperous: there was the Presi-
dential reward to be divided.

On May 22nd, Davis was in Virginia's Fortress Monroe—"that living

tomb," as it was called by the New York *Herald*, which continued, not omitting to gloat over the libel of women's dress: "No more will Jeff Davis be known among the masses of men. . . . His life has been a cheat. His last free act was an effort to unsex himself, and deceive the world. He keeps the character, we may say, in death, and is buried alive." His cell was a specially prepared casemate of the fortress, with the water, at high tide, coming almost to the sill of the barred window. Within a grated door, two armed sentries were stationed, with two others just outside, and in that outer room an officer under orders to inspect the captive every quarter hour. The outer room was, in turn, secured by an outside lock, the key in the hands of the commanding officer of the guard, and the locked door under the immediate guard of two more sentries. Sentries, closely stationed, guarded all approaches to the region of the casemate, and there were similar sentry lines on the outside parapet and directly across on the glacis of the moat. A guardroom was established to each side of the prisoner's casemate, in which a lamp burned perpetually.

There Davis awaited the will of three men: President Johnson, Secretary of War Edwin M. Stanton, and General Nelson A. Miles, who commanded the fortress. As for the first, Johnson, illiterate until after his marriage, had not only a hatred of the class to which Davis had ascended but a personal resentment against Davis, who he felt had once insulted him in the Senate by a reference to tailors, Johnson having been a tailor before entering politics. To make matters worse, at the formal celebration in Washington when Richmond fell (Lincoln already on his visit there), Johnson, as Vice-President, on the speakers' platform, answered a patriotic voice from the crowd that yelled for the hanging of Jeff Davis by bursting out, "Yes, I say hang him twenty times!" He would, he added, hang them all. Secretary Stanton had been the presence behind the medievally brutal tortures of the as yet unconvicted accused at the trial after Lincoln's death—a legal procedure that remains a blot on American history.

Stanton now expected, apparently, to try Davis in the same fashion. General Miles had risen, with four wounds in action, from captain to major general of volunteers. The wounds had helped, no doubt, but Miles had learned that valor and merit could be supplemented by skillful respect for and connivance with authority. Stanton's department had directed that the prisoner should be put in irons if Miles thought it necessary. Miles immediately took the subtle suggestion. The ascent even of merit can be greased, and he was to become Major General Miles of the regular Army; a little later, he married a niece of Sherman; eventually, he became commander-in-chief of the Army, following such stars as Grant, Sherman, and Sheridan; he died at a circus performance and, to complete the comedy, was buried in a hero's tomb at Arlington.

A slight difficulty was encountered, however, in the fettering of Davis. A captain entered the casemate, followed by two men holding a length of chain with shackles. There is some discrepancy in reports of the ensuing dialogue, but the captain later wrote a letter concerning the event. Upon Davis's asking if he was to be shackled, the captain replied that such were his orders. Davis said, "Those are orders for a slave, and no man with a soul in him would obey such orders." Upon the captain's reiteration of his orders, Davis said, "I shall never submit to such an indignity." When a demand to see General Miles was refused, Davis said, "Let your men shoot me at once." In the end, it took four men to overpower the prisoner and flatten him on his cot for the fettering. Like Black Hawk, years earlier, Davis evidently preferred death to dishonor, but neither man was allowed the option.

Secretary Stanton was having his way. What Lincoln's way would have been is suggested by his answer, toward the end of the war, to a question about what fate awaited Davis. Lincoln began the tale of an Irishman who had signed the temperance pledge but later wondered if any harm would be done if he happened to take on a couple "unbeknownst to himself." Then, no doubt after a pause, Lincoln wondered what harm would be done if Davis slipped out of the country "unbeknownst" to him.

The torments went on—chiefly the ever-lighted lamp and the never-ending tread of the guard, which forbade sleep. The tale of the shackling was grist for the journalistic mill, but some resentment on the part of readers began to replace applause. Meanwhile, the one person of humane instincts with whom Davis came into contact was the prison doctor, John C. Craven, whose duty was presumably to preserve life in the body for the further torture of a military trial. Dr. Craven, who later wrote a book on Davis, saw the shackles as nothing but a danger to the survival of his charge, and as a result of his intervention—as well as some backfire from public opinion— they were removed after five days. Craven saw that the allaying of "cerebral excitement" was the first thing to consider in the condition of his patient, and when Craven found that a guard had laid claim to Davis's pipe as a souvenir he provided pipe and tobacco. But Craven had trouble procuring changes of clothing for Davis at proper intervals—a fact that he regarded for Davis as "unmerited insult heaped on helplessness"—and with difficulty got him heavy underwear and a coat for winter. Only after a long period could he procure proper facilities and, finally, a change of quarters for the prisoner, who suffered from the dampness of the moat. Davis's blind eye—blind for years now—prompted him, according to Craven's account, to reach back into his memory for Milton:

> Oh dark, dark, dark, amid the
>   blaze of noon;
> Irrevocably dark, total eclipse
>   without the hope of day.

And:

>   Yet I argue not
> Against Heaven's hand or will, nor
>   bate a jot
> Of heart or hope: but still bear up
>   and steer
> Right onward.

It was just as well that Davis, in the lonely years of reading and study, had stocked his mind, and could find his heart spoken for him in lines like Milton's, for he was allowed no books (except the Prayer Book and the Bible) and, of course, no newspapers. Craven wrote that "except for the purpose of petty torture there could be no color of reason for withholding" such items. But the greatest torture of all was the denial of communication between the prisoner and members of his family, who were now forbidden to leave Savannah, where they were friendless, but where Varina did her best, by correspondence, to excite a sense of justice for her husband. Meanwhile, bad health, especially erysipelas, weakened Davis—illness brought on chiefly, Dr. Craven reported, by the fear that he might die "without opportunity of rebutting in public trial" the charge of conspiracy to assassinate Lincoln. The will of Davis, his self-control, piety, generosity of spirit, and refusal to blame others won Craven's admiration and heart. "Mr. Davis is remarkable for the kindliness of his nature and fidelity to friends," he wrote. Elsewhere, he wrote that "there were moments . . . in which Mr. Davis impressed me more than any professor of Christianity I had ever heard." And "Let me here remark that, despite a certain exterior cynicism of manner, no patient has ever crossed my path who, suffering so much himself, appeared to feel so warmly and tenderly for others."

Over this period hung the grim image of what the farcical military trial and accompanying tortures for the plotters (and others) of Lincoln's assassination had been. But the pendulum had begun to swing back. The London *Times* had come out for clemency, not because of sympathy for Davis but for the sake of the American Union. And as the state of affairs at Fortress Monroe became better known, and the early public approval began to fade, influential Northern lawyers, no secessionists but honest men devoted to the cause of law and justice—including Charles O'Conor, a nationally recognized ornament of the bar—began scrupulously to study the case. O'Conor wrote a letter to Davis, which did not reach the hands of the addressee until it had passed through those of General Miles, who, still eager to please, consulted higher authority before giving Davis permission to reply. All sorts of difficulties were made; O'Conor and others of repute were refused admittance to Davis (who, having no newspapers, could know nothing of what was going on). But meanwhile an irremediable split had now occurred between the vengeful President and the Republicans. For instance, even Representative Thaddeus Stevens, an advocate of stern Reconstruction policies, offered—no doubt for political purposes of his own—to become one of the defenders of Davis.

To complicate matters, Chief Justice Salmon P. Chase, a well-known opponent of slavery, had declared that to try Davis for treason would be to condemn the North publicly, for by the Constitution itself, he said, secession was not treason. This would mean that the vindictive government would risk having the Supreme Court declare that the victors had waged war illegally. Worse was to come. When the easy way out seemed to be for a number of prominent men to support a petition to get Davis a pardon, which, if granted, would get the President and others off the hook, Davis was determined to let them hang there. To ask for a pardon was, he said, an admission of guilt, and he refused to put his name to the document. The trial was what he wanted, and the outcome of the trial seemed ever more certain as his indefatigable defenders found evidence of the government's intention to try to connect Davis with poor Henry Wirz, the commandant of Andersonville prison, who was executed under the accusation of having starved his prisoners. The intention to connect Davis with Wirz was based on hope and delusion. (The defenders had already carefully considered all possible evidence on this point.)

In spite of discomfiture, the government continued its tough policy, and forbade conferences between Davis and counsel, at the same time trying to agitate the old question of the embezzlement of the remains of the Confederate Treasury. And, in a last act of desperation, the private correspondence of the lawyers supporting Davis was seized and tampered with. Yet the idea of a military trial appeared more and more dangerous from the political point of view.

All this time, the light in the cell was kept burning, and Mrs. Davis, without formal accusation of any kind, was held prisoner within the limits of Savannah, and not even allowed to visit Augusta, where she might have had the comfort of family. In addition, she had to endure the humiliation of seeing published extracts ("garbled," according to her account) of letters to and from her husband found in their baggage by the original hunters for the Confederate treasure. By August of 1865, however, she had been allowed to go to New York, and had been welcomed there by George Shea, the first lawyer to undertake her husband's defense. Clearly, the atmosphere was, under new influences, changing. Davis was allowed to receive the Confederate General J. Brown Gordon, who later said, from a public platform, that he had seen Davis in victory at the First Manassas and that "the vicarious sufferer" for his people locked in Fortress Monroe "was greater and grander still in the hour of his deepest humiliation."

The confusion in government circles was indicated by the fact that in May of 1866 an indictment was handed up against Davis in the Circuit Court of Norfolk. (Originally, Lee was also to have been indicted, but Grant protested that Lee was protected by the parole Grant had received.) The government seemed to have forgotten that a trial was exactly what Davis and his lawyers most wanted. Then, mysteriously, the record of the indictment was lost.

Later that month, Mrs. Davis succeeded in gaining an interview with President Johnson, whose mendacity and evasiveness reached monumental heights, and who, grasping at a straw, himself suggested that all would be solved if Davis would only ask for a pardon. The answer was predictable. Chief Justice Chase, who had originally advised against futile prosecution for treason, accepted a suggestion that Davis might get bail by having some such important person as Horace Greeley—an enemy turned friend for the sake of justice, he was already a stout defender of Davis—sign the bail bond. Mrs. Davis presented the case to Greeley, who not only agreed to sign the bond but eloquently fought, through his paper, for an immediate trial.

In the meantime, the rigors of prison had been relaxed (General Miles was assigned to another post), but the whole affair seemed again bogged down in political considerations and incompetence—or subject to undefinable forces. In the end, however, under the various pressures that had been accumulating, the District Court in Richmond issued a writ of habeas corpus directing the commandant of Fortress Monroe to "present the body" of the accused. On May 12, 1867, in Richmond, Mr. and Mrs. Davis occupied the same rooms at the Spotswood Hotel as on his arrival as President of the Confederate States of America. The next day, after William M. Evarts, soon to be the Attorney General of the United States, had announced that the case was not to be raised at "the present term," a bail bond was signed by ten men, including Horace Greeley, Cornelius Vanderbilt (by proxy), and—most fantastic of all—Gerrit Smith. Smith, an ardent abolitionist and one of the Secret Six who had backed John Brown for the raid on Harpers Ferry, later wrote, concerning his present motives: "I have ever held that a sufficient reason why we should not punish the conquered South is that the North was quite as responsible as the South for the chief cause of the war . . . the mercenary North coolly reckoned the political, commercial, and ecclesiastical profits of slavery, and held to it."

Davis had come out of the war with popularity diminished almost to the vanishing point, but when, free on bail, he emerged from the courthouse in Richmond, the rebel yell burst forth for the first time since the last few Southern bayonets had glittered in a futile charge. Back at the apartment in the Spotswood Hotel, Davis, his wife, and Dr. Charles Francis Minnegerode, his rector, retired into an inner room and knelt in prayer.

The general situation in which Davis found himself was anomalous. He had been freed on bail by a civil court, with the implication, warranted by the President and the Chief Justice, that the law of peace prevailed. But Congress maintained that the South was still legally in a state of rebellion. Not able to pursue the hope of occupying a useful position in his own land while the indictment stood, and pursued, as he wrote, by "a spirit of vengeful persecution," Davis still held his ground in refusing to consider any plan that involved the application for a pardon. His attitude was clearly stated by James Redpath—the same James Redpath who had been an ardent abolitionist in "Bleeding Kansas," who, as a daring reporter, had sought out and interviewed John Brown in his hideaway after the Pottawatomie Massacre, who had written the first, and frantically laudatory, biography of Brown ("The Public Life of Captain John Brown"), and who had termed him a

"Warrior Saint" and a "warrior of the Lord and of Gideon." Now, years later, a somewhat more realistic reporter, he sought out another flinty old man, whom he described as "a statesman with clean hands and pure heart." In summary, Redpath said of Davis, "He was true, all his life long, to the creed in which he had been reared; and hence it was impossible for him to 'repent and recant.' He could not repent of being honest, or recant what he believed to be true." Davis had written, in fact, to the chairman of the congressional Committee on Amnesty that he did not wish any bill under its consideration to be endangered because he might be included in its provisions. Amnesty, like pardon, implied crime, and he admitted none.

Because of his legal situation, Davis had refused the presidency of Randolph-Macon College, as he had refused offers amounting to charity. His lawyers suggested that he travel abroad and investigate business connections, but Canada, England, and France provided no openings, in spite of the fact that, especially in England, Davis was received with hospitality in certain aristocratic circles—a hospitality of which he could not avail himself, because his wife's pride would not allow her to appear in her church-mouse poverty. Returning to America, where he encountered other disappointments, including the project of a railroad to California, he finally became president of the Carolina Life Insurance Company, with headquarters at Memphis, but this project failed, costing Davis his capital of fifteen thousand dollars. To compound his desperate situation, his ownership of Brierfield came into litigation (with kinspeople), because Joseph, now dead, had not technically transferred ownership to his brother. The property did finally come to Davis, but the war had left it drastically devalued.

Nor had the dogged political persecutors quite given up. The old indictment was now revised by the federal government to place him in a group of presumptive conspirators, including Robert E. Lee, the hope being that Lee (how little they could have understood his old-fashioned sense of decency!) would try to exculpate himself by what would amount to turning state's evidence against his superior. The whole indictment was based on the assumption that, as Lincoln had originally declared, the war was merely a "domestic insurrection"—not a civil war. Davis, as before, was eager for a trial.

In a tragicomic sequel, however, the new indictment was quashed by a provision of the Fourteenth Amendment which imposed perpetual disenfranchisement on anyone who aided in rebellion after having taken the oath of certain offices. Unquestionably, Davis, who had twice been inducted into the Senate, was already "suffering" under just such a disability, and to demand further punishment would involve double jeopardy, forbidden by the Constitution. On this ground, an action to quash the indictment against Davis was heard on December 3, 1868, in the United States Circuit Court of Virginia, with Chief Justice Chase on the bench with Justice John Curtiss Underwood. When Justice Underwood refused to quash the indictment, the Chief Justice entered a dissent, and the case was dropped as of December 5, 1868.

Poor Davis was never to have the day in court that he yearned for in order to justify his public career. What was left was a protracted and increasingly bitter quarrel with his old enemy General Joseph E. Johnston, C.S.A., and others, and his struggle to survive. He wanted to survive to write his book on the Confederacy. There seemed a widespread willingness to provide him with information and documents, but leisure and a quiet place to work were lacking. Fortunately, a widow by the name of Mrs. Sarah A. Dorsey, who held Confederate views and had preserved some wealth, offered Davis a cottage on her estate, Beauvoir, on the Mississippi coast near Biloxi, at just enough rent to salve his pride. But Varina, though she had been a childhood friend of Mrs. Dorsey, now jealously loathed the lady, who not only urged her husband on with his book but devoted herself to him as a secretary; the loathing was so great that for many months Varina would not even visit her husband at the cottage, preferring to stay in Memphis. Only after Davis had agreed to go with her away from Beauvoir did she, with female prerogative, change her mind and join him there. By her husband's offer, she had, we may surmise, made good the priority of claim to his company. Davis proceeded with "The Rise and Fall of the Confederate Government," and it appeared in 1881—a work primarily of legalistic and constitutional apologetics, and not at all the narrative that the title promised and the world expected. Abstract concerns had swallowed the tragic drama. The book was, in short, a failure—practically and otherwise. To further depress the author, the son who was his namesake, born in 1857, failed to pass his examinations at the Virginia Military Institute and was dismissed.

The only comfort that came to Davis after the failure of the book was the fact that Mrs. Dorsey, aware of Varina's jealousy, sold him, cheaply and on long terms, Beauvoir itself, so that the husband and wife could be reunited. This kindness was compounded—or perhaps complicated—when, shortly afterward, Mrs. Dorsey died and her will was opened. It named Davis not only as her executor but as her heir. It would be interesting to know all the psychological ins and outs of this situation. But in any case Davis now had a home.

He was also soon to have a home in the hearts of his people. The rancor, blame, charges of tyranny, and criticism (justified and unjustified) directed at him as a natural consequence of defeat were dying away. In 1886, he was invited to Montgomery to be the guest of honor at the unveiling of a monument to the Confederate dead, near the old capitol, where Davis had been designated President of the new nation. At first, he declined, but in the end he went, with wildly enthusiastic crowds greeting his special railroad car all along the route—crowds far greater than on that other trip, in 1861, when he had left Brierfield to assume his tragic role at Montgomery. Now, again at Montgomery, he was conducted, under a drizzle, through an undeterred throng of fifteen thousand enraptured spectators, to the same hotel as in 1861—the Exchange Hotel (now operated by a Bostonian, with decorations overseen by a wounded Union veteran)—and, under a barrage of flowers, to the same quarters he had originally occupied there, Room 101, where the walls to each side of the door were draped with the national flag but with a portrait of Lee hung above. The quilt on the bed was one under which Lafayette had once slept.

After Montgomery, other cities claimed the ritual presence. The story was repeated. As a symbol of irrepressible principle, as the vicarious sufferer for his people, as the image of honor, Davis entered the hearts of his countrymen, to be called from city to city the eternal President of the City of the Soul into which the human disorder of the Confederate States of America had been mystically converted.

There was one poor casualty in the midst of the glory. Davis's daughter Winnie (Varina Anne Jefferson Davis), now with her own burden of symbolism as "the Daughter of the Confederacy," fell in love with a young man named Alfred Wilkinson. A successful lawyer in Syracuse, New York, he was refined, well educated, a gentleman with every virtue, every grace. He was a grandson of the Reverend Mr. Samuel J. May, an abolitionist, but now Wilkinson was visiting Beauvoir, where he was received with the utmost hospitality. He had come to ask for Winnie's hand, but how could Davis accept him as a son-in-law? How could the Daughter of the Confederacy betray her constituency? Winnie bowed to her father's wishes. Davis, forgetting the passion that he and little Knox Taylor had known—and the passion that he and Varina had shared, and all the illusions of love that surpass reality—entered his world of private abstraction. He died shortly thereafter, on December 6, 1889. Winnie fell into a decline, never knew love again, took to writing novels and biographies, and died on September 18, 1898, at the age of thirty-four, perhaps the last casualty of the Civil War.

WHEN Davis was in his last illness, a movement was initiated in Congress to revoke the civil disabilities that his career had earned him, but a combination of old rancor and political timidity prevailed, even though a poll among Union veterans who had heard the rebel yell and survived showed that they, at least, were beyond rancor or political calculation. In 1975, citizenship was finally restored to Lee. The following year, on January 25th, Senator Mark Hatfield, of Oregon, introduced Senate Joint Resolution 16, to return citizenship to Jefferson Davis, in order to right, as he put it, a "glaring injustice in the history of the United States." Hatfield quoted the words of Chief Justice Chase: "If you bring these leaders to trial, it will condemn the North, for by the Constitution secession is not rebellion. We cannot convict him of treason." And the Senator continued with a quotation from Davis, saying, "In his memoirs, Davis declared it his purpose to 'keep the memory of our Southern heroes green, for they belong not to us alone: they belong to the whole country: they belong to America.'" Hatfield added, "I seek to keep his memory green, and to restore to him the rights due an outstanding American." The resolution passed unanimously, by voice vote, and, on October 17, 1978, was signed into law by President Carter.

It cannot be said that enthusiasm for keeping the memory of the "outstanding American" green swept the country. The event made at best a brief news note on a back page—except, that is, in Todd County, Kentucky, where Davis was born. And even there, no doubt, the enthusiasm, in the face of inflation and gasoline prices and the struggle for daily bread, was generally confined to the local historical society, the United Daughters of the

Confederacy, the Jefferson Davis Birthplace Association, and a hard core of civic-minded citizens.

The little park, of course, had already been established, and in 1924 the obelisk had been completed and, on June 7th, dedicated. The replica of the partly clapboarded log cabin of Samuel Davis had been dedicated October 17th of that year. The dedication of the monument had apparently given occasion for a rural festival, scarcely noticed in the press, but when, not long afterward, I revisited the site, bearing with me some vestiges of the near-forgotten puzzlement provoked by the old man under the cedar tree, it was a deserted spot with a struggling greensward, marked here and there by thistle and mullein, facing a street of rather unpretentious and sometimes decrepit houses.

This was the picture I had carried in my head over half a dozen years of absence. On returning to the region, I remember, I was able to see to the north, from certain points on the highway between my home town and Hopkinsville, the seat of Christian County, a faint white finger pointing skyward. Occasionally, I wondered, with some sort of embarrassed irony, what Jefferson Davis would have thought if he had known that in December of 1923, as the monument was nearing completion, the Ku Klux Klan had been allowed to burn a great cross above the structure being reared in his honor. In justice, I should add that that was the only activity in Todd County of the Klan in my memory, though in the violent period after the Civil War the region around Fairview had been rather notable for the strength of the organization. And I never knew of any Klan performances in my natal section, the two lynchings I can think of that took place there being of a more informal order.

THE celebration of the restoration of Jefferson Davis's citizenship was set for May 31, 1979, and the first three days of June, June 3rd being the birthday of the county's most famous citizen. In Todd County, the atmosphere of celebration was thickened by the fact that June 2nd was the centennial of the official founding of the town of Guthrie. So there was both competition and fusion in the festivities of the week.

The preface to the main event concerning Davis—the celebration of his birthday on June 3rd—was in the form of a drama presenting the more significant events of the life of the subject, from childhood to the release from prison. The script was prepared by Rebecca Williams and Mary Helen Adams, citizens of Hopkinsville with dramatic ambition and gifts, and presented by the Pennyrile Players (Pennyroyal being the name of that region of the state). Interspersed between scenes of immediate dramatic interest were lyrics and ballads to give atmosphere or provide information not suitable for direct handling. The stage was set up on an asphalt parking area some distance behind the monument, in an area with enough slope to afford good visibility for spectators. The stage itself was in three sections, the first (stage right) and the third (stage left) being four or five feet from ground level, and the middle amost at ground level—an arrangement that worked well to provide a fluid continuity of action when that was desirable. The back wall of the first section was painted to resemble masonry (as for the cell in Fortress Monroe); the second was backed by a dark-red fabric of no particular definition; and the third was furnished as a kind of drawing room, with period portraits on the walls, and windows painted on to give an impression of distance beyond. Before each of the performances (on three successive nights), eight young men, four in Confederate gray and four in Union blue, bearing arms, marched back and forth across the rear of the area of seating in the open-air theatre.

The presentations went forward against certain difficulties. Rain had interfered with rehearsals; in fact, the opening of the play was the first dress rehearsal. As for costumes, marks of military rank were sometimes a hodge-podge; for instance, the rating on the sleeve of Davis as a cadet at West Point was the same as that on the sleeve of his instructor. More important—though this problem was to an extent ingeniously remedied by the Pennyrile Players—was the State Department of Parks' failure (or so it was reported) to make good on the promise of a stage with proper lighting and sound equipment. There was an excess of sound in a few respects: in non-battle scenes an almost constant effect of musketry was achieved by a busy machine for popping corn; in addition, certain members of the Pennyrile Players who were not in the present production entered into enthusiastic discussion of one in which they were to participate—"Oklahoma!" There was, of course, the usual quota of young children crunching bags of potato chips, giggling, punching each other, dragging chairs about, and otherwise delighting their parents.

On the first night, in spite of the valiant and not untalented work of the cast—especially of Paul Meier, who played the character of Jefferson Davis—the reception was, though not tepid, short of an ovation. That night, the audience totalled about a hundred, including twenty-odd grade-school children (probably dragged there against their will), a few teen-agers, and forty-odd spectators well into middle age, with the remainder between twenty-five and forty. To judge from the license plates in the parking lot, a considerable majority of the audience was from Christian County, the home of the Pennyrile Players, and there was only one person identifiably from Guthrie (which was no doubt bemused by its own celebration). In general, the audience seemed to be middle-class, with a generous sprinkling of professional people. As might have been expected from the subject, there were no blacks in the audience—though there was one on the stage.

The second performance, on June 1st, drew a somewhat larger audience, although children, like the hero of the play, seemed to have been vigorous in asserting their constitutional rights and had stayed at home, and teen-agers, few the night before, had almost reached the vanishing point, too. But citizens of Guthrie had increased by a hundred per cent: there were two. The audience, now predominantly middle-aged, did make effective protest about the offstage musketry, but when this was quieted some brass-bellied bullfrogs took over, like drunken brigadiers giving incoherent orders from a dugout—an occurrence not unknown to the Civil War. There was also an increase in appreciation the second night—in fact, an ovation.

But the commemoration of the valor and steadfastness of Jefferson Davis did not end with that. Once the not large audience had cleared away, there was a

celebration more to the public taste—
and one that might have been more to
the taste of the young lieutenant who
once swirled the lissome squaw into
a waltz. A square dance began on
the blacktop to the left of the monument. The dancers, generally clothed
in jeans and tank tops, were the young
set who had been absent from the play
that night, and who would also be absent from the more serious celebration
of the birthday. And why not? Had
Jefferson Davis earlier been more than
a name to most of them—if that?
Mixed with the young were a few elderly couples, seeming out of place,
whether they knew about Jefferson
Davis or not. But they did know about
the calls and the figures; probably they
were square-dance buffs, drawn to any
event that might provide dancing.

The third night was a disaster. The
audience, probably because of word-of-
mouth advertising, had increased to
about two hundred, the majority now
with raincoats or umbrellas, for the
sky was lowering. The most Spartan
and patriotic stayed on after rain began, among them an elderly couple
with a black poodle that sat on its master's lap and paid close attention. The

rain grew worse. Last-ditchers huddled under plastic or under a quilt snatched from an early scene. But they, too, were forced to retreat, and the play was called. In the protection of one of the improvised shelters, a stocky twenty-year-old—why there to begin with, God knows—kept wishing he was home with TV and a case of beer handy. Put yourself in his place, and be not one to cast the first stone when the rain beats down on Kentucky. On this third night, after the downpour had passed, the Jefferson Davis Ball took place at the Todd County Central High School, in Elkton, the county seat (a rather charming old town, not yet undone by time and progress). The inclement weather had its effect. Only twenty-five couples turned up (maintaining their courage, no doubt, from brown paper sacks containing bottles). The dancers scarcely outnumbered the orchestra provided for the occasion.

Another celebration—of the centennial of the founding of Guthrie—had occurred earlier in the day. It included, among various events, one from near-pioneer days—a demonstration of old-fashioned soapmaking. Above this activity hung a copy of a handed-down "re-ceet" giving full information for "clothes bilin":

1. Bild fire in backyard to het kettle of rain water.
2. Set tubs so smoke won't blow in eyes if wind is pert.
3. Shave 1 hole cake of lie sope in bilin water.
4. Sort things. Make three piles, 1 pile white, 1 pile cullord, 1 pile britches and rags.
5. Stur flour in cold water to smooth, then thin down with bilin water.
6. Rub dirty spots on board. Scrub hard. Then bile. Rub cullord but don't bile. Just rench and starch.
7. Take white things out of kettle with broom handel, rench, then blew and starch.
8. Spred tee towels on grass.
9. Hang old rags on fence.
10. Pour rench water in flowerbed.
11. Scrub porch with sopy water.
12. Turn tubs upside down.
13. Go put on clean dress. Smooth hair with side combs, brew cup of tea, set and rest and rock a spell and count blessins.

Perhaps the only direction still relevant is "count blessins." But in our day and time, for too many reasons to enumerate, that direction, too, may be antiquated.

The main event of the afternoon was to be a historical parade, ar-

ranged by one of the most highly regarded citizens of the region, an efficient, handsome, witty man, married
to a very attractive and very blond
young woman. He is the great-grand-
son of a Comanche chief and is usually called Nick, for the simple reason
that his real name is unpronounce-
able by most Todd County tongues.
Nick is noted for his public spirit. A
trained emergency medical technician
in a doctorless community, he is a
member of the Todd County Rescue
Squad, and is on call day and night,
without pay. Now, as master of the
parade, he wanted to get an antiquated
farm wagon, with appropriate mules,
to be driven by a certain grizzled old
black of the outlying country, himself
a relic of another era. The old man he
wanted lived some seven miles away,
and was of years uncountable. He was,
he said, getting too old to be bothered
by such goings on. But the old-fashioned black man had an afterthought.
He said he might do it after all—if he
had that stuff that used to come sealed
up in a quart fruit jar and looked like
water but wasn't. The master of the
parade, thinking how long it had been
since the repeal of the Volstead Act,

was hard put to it. But he proposed a compromise: "Would some of that store-bought stuff that comes in a big, flat bottle, brown, not white, and stuck in a brown paper bag, the kind of stuff white folks drinks—would that do?" After weighing the question, the old man said yes, it would do. If it held as much as a quart jar. I am not informed what hand passed the brown paper sack, but it was passed. Then on the great day, unpredictably—or predictably—after several nips from the bottle in the brown paper bag the mule driver, at a crucial point in the parade, dropped reins, stopped, lifted the bag, and held it high for a long time. The mules, meanwhile, had ventured, of their own accord, toward the railroad tracks. It took great powers of persuasion on the part of the Comanche, along with physical strength, to get things back in order.

June 3rd, the birthday, to be commemorated by more serious proceedings than even the drama and the ball, dawned unseasonably cool, with overcast skies, but it cleared later. Above the gateway to the little park hung the flags of the United States, the Confederacy, and the Commonwealth of

Kentucky. The base of the monument served as a platform, and the railings of the fourteen steps leading to it were draped with red-white-and-blue bunting. At 1 P.M., with an audience mostly in "church clothes," in contrast to the casual attire at the dramatic productions, the commemoration opened. On the platform were various dignitaries, including the president of the Todd County Historical Society, the president of the Kentucky Historical Society, the curator of the museums and shrines of the Kentucky Department of Parks, the president of the Jefferson Davis Birthplace Association, David Wright, who had placed the bronze cap on the peak of the monument back in 1924, and the speaker of the occasion—Dr. Holman Hamilton, professor of history emeritus at the University of Kentucky. A letter of regret from President Carter at not being able to attend and speak was read, as was a statement he made on signing the document that returned citizenship to Davis. Dr. Hamilton included in his main address a quotation from Davis blessing Kentucky on his last visit to Fairview, in 1886. And so the ceremony ended.

IT is a rainy morning in late August. I want to stand before the monument to see it rear, as years before, blank and lonely against the sky. There is no person in sight—none near the towering obelisk. And there is nobody beneath that structure. On December 11, 1889, in New Orleans, a hearse, drawn by black horses, bearing a now whittled-down and nearly weightless human burden, had led the longest funeral procession ever seen in that city out to the Metaire Cemetery. But the last tribute was to be a struggle among states for possession of the trivial remains of a man who in life had known as much revilement as honor. Now Kentucky claimed a son and Georgia a grandson, while Montgomery, the seat of the founding of the Confederacy, gave Alabama a claim. But Virginia quite properly won the contest, for it was here, in Richmond, that Davis had endured his fame and his tragedy. So on May 31, 1893, with full military honors, the body of the President of the Confederacy was reinterred in Hollywood Cemetery— with what comic irony in that name of the cemetery, so appropriate to "Gone with the Wind." As a less comic irony, we may remember that the body now lay on the banks of the James River, where an America was born that the dead man had outlived.

That morning, last August, I had already stood beside occupied graves, some miles southward of Fairview. My brother and I—wordless, as usual on such occasions—had observed the graves of our parents, then of his first wife, and then of one of the two persons who had been my closest friends in boyhood, the one who had been my tutor in boyish woodcraft, and who, through short years of greatness and long years of failure, had remained a friend. Then my brother said, "I've tried to find out all I can down here about Old Jeff"—the one who had trodden the crossties with his croker sack on his way to town to do his "Sat'dy traden." Nobody, my brother added, knew where he had come from. It seemed that he had just suddenly appeared as what he was.

"But he's over there now in the potter's field," my brother said—an unmowed strip of weeds and grass near the railroad, where the heavy freights groaned up a long grade eastward. And there, too, was the grave of

Old Jeff's wife, the tombstone the handiwork of the bereaved, twisted old husband, the town's feckless jack-of-all-trades, whose grief-stricken masterpiece was scarcely a masterpiece. He had obviously first made a wooden box, some twenty inches by thirty, and about five inches deep, then filled it with cement, probably bracing it with scraps of chickenwire. At last, before the cement had really hardened, he had, with some blunt blade, scratched on an epitaph. It said, with brute economy of language and space:

GONE
 TO REST

MANDY
DAVIS

BORN APRIL
 17–1877

DIED JULY
 23–1941

Beside the crank-sided slab was a neater little stone, commercial-made —the kind a grateful government sets up to commemorate its penniless veteran. From it I learned that Old Jeff, too, had served his country, at the time of the Spanish-American War and a little thereafter. In heroism or in quaking fear—it is not recorded.

As for the great monument of the other Jeff Davis, who had received enemy lead into his own body and continued to sit his mount while a boot filled with blood, it stood there blank, whiter now after a refurbishing for the commemoration: preternaturally white against the slow, curdling grayness of clouding sky, and somehow, suddenly, meaningless.

The growth of thistle and mullein, the discarded planks, the random shacks of the process of building, the scrabble pastures stretching into distance—all the things I remembered from boyhood had changed. The modest park is now green and is mowed with official efficiency. It is a rectangle something more than a city block wide and two or three long, reaching into the straggling settlement. A few abandoned and decaying frame houses face the park, and on the street along one side are several boxlike, tidy little white houses of recent vintage and one great chunk of a reddish brick building, two stories high or more, ugly, looking out of place. It was built after the monument, I learned, and was once the schoolhouse but is now the Arm of the Lord Trinity Pentecostal Church, staring across at the worldly glory and vainglory of an ex-Baptist turned Episcopalian. A couple of buildings down the main street stands a rather handsome, well-maintained old white farmhouse, and beyond it the fields stretch westward away into the fertile green of Christian County.

I wander back into the park. The drizzle has ceased, but now and then a drop falling from a higher vantage point makes its hollow resonance on a stout oak leaf. Over to one side, slick with wet, a few painted metal seesaws, slides, and swings look out of place in the almost rural setting. But no doubt in bright summer weather, when cars pull in bearing all kinds of license plates and carrying passengers who know, by and large, as little about the history of the nation as about the difference between the doctrine of transubstantiation and that of consubstantiation, and when candy wrappers and lunch wrappers spot the officially mowed grass, some children do find use for the swings and seesaws.

Then, no doubt, the spirit of the man to whom the monument is erected, wherever and whatever it may be, may look down with pleasure on the gaiety of children; for, in spite of all rigidity of character, stiffness of dignity, abstract logicality, and locked-in personality, he had a simple affection for the very young and naturally won their confidence. More wryly, perhaps, he looks down on the well-meant and ignorant charade honoring his sufferings and triumphs.

Davis died without rancor, and wishing us all well. But if he were not now defenseless in death, he would no doubt reject the citizenship we so charitably thrust upon him. In life, in his old-fashioned way, he would accept no pardon, for pardon could be construed to imply wrongdoing, and wrongdoing was what, in honor and principle, he denied. (As did Lee, quite specifically.) So he holds eternal franchise in that shadowy, ages-ago-established, rarely remembered nation of men and women who in their brief lives learned the true definition of honor, far beyond the triviality of the code duello once defended by the young Davis.

Some historians say that with Appomattox the "business ethic" became triumphant in American life, and that common speech reflects the notion. "Mr. Smith," we say, "is worth a million dollars": Mr. Smith is no longer a person—he is a million dollars. Suppose that Lincoln, who, some historians say, scarcely understood the world he helped to bring to birth, or even the fuddled Grant, who after the farce of his Presidency and his idiotic business operations redeemed himself in his final days of lonely suffering and honor—suppose Lincoln or Grant should have citizenship thrust upon him by the America of today. Would either happily accept citizenship in a nation that sometimes seems technologically and philosophically devoted to the depersonalization of men? In a way, in their irrefrangible personal identity, Lincoln and Grant were almost as old-fashioned as Jefferson Davis.

MEANWHILE, some of us may now and then look up at the obelisk in Todd County, white against sunny or cloudy sky, and remember what Herodotus of Halicarnassus, the first historian, said of his purpose in writing—in creating the first great verbal monument: ". . . that the great deeds of men may not be forgotten . . . whether Greek or foreigners; and especially the causes of their wars."